Like ou.
@RiddlesandGiggles

Follow us on Instagram
@RiddlesandGiggles_Official

Questions & Customer Service
hello@riddlesandgiggles.com

Thanksgiving Joke Book for Kids

by Riddles and Giggles™

www.riddlesandgiggles.com

© 2021 Riddles and Giggles™

All rights reserved. This book or parts thereof may not be reproduced in any form, stored in any retrieval system, or transmitted in any form by any means—electronic, mechanical, photocopy, recording, or otherwise—without prior written permission of the publisher, except as provided by United States of America copyright law. For permissions contact: hello@riddlesandgiggles.com

Not for resale. All books, digital products, eBooks and PDF downloads are subject to copyright protection. Each book, eBook and PDF download is licensed to a single user only. Customers are not allowed to copy, distribute, share and/or transfer the product they have purchased to any third party.

RIDDLES & GIGGLES

FREE BONUS

Get your FREE book download

Christmas Jokes & Would You Rather for Kids

- Contains a collection of cracking Christmas jokes and Would You Rather Christmas-themed questions

- More endless giggles and entertainment for the whole family.

Claim your FREE book at www.riddlesandagiggles.com/christmas

Or scan with your phone to get your free download

TABLE OF CONTENTS

Welcome 4

Tips on How To Tell a Joke 5

Fun Ideas for Thanksgiving Day 5

   1. Turkey Jokes 7

   2. Thanksgiving Origins & Traditions 17

   3. Thanksgiving Food & Celebrations 25

   4. Thanksgiving Knock Knock Jokes 37

   5. Thanksgiving Puns & One-Liners 49

   6. Fall Jokes 55

   7. Fall Knock Knock Jokes 59

   8. Fall Puns & One-Liners 65

Before You Go 71

References 102

WELCOME

Hi there, Jokester!

Jokes are a great way for people to have fun and share laughs together.

Lots of people love to tell jokes. Some are very funny. Some are just corny. Other jokes make no sense at all. One thing we can agree on about jokes is that kids love them!

I hope you are one of those kids, because if you want a collection of funny, corny, and laugh-out-loud jokes, this book is for you!

The *Thanksgiving Joke Book for Kids* is an excellent collection of good, clean, fun jokes that will make you roll your eyes, snort, giggle, groan, and laugh out loud.

You can read this whole book or pick which jokes you want to read in any order you want.

You can also enjoy reading the jokes on your own or share the jokes with everyone around you. You can also take turns reading the jokes out loud with family and friends.

PSST... You can also color the Thanksgiving pictures and use this book as a coloring book AND a joke book!

Fun Ideas for Thanksgiving Day

Before we get to the jokes, here are a few ways you can add some giggles and laughs to your Thanksgiving celebrations.

Make joke napkin rings! Cut strips of paper (about 2 inches x 5 inches) and write jokes on them. Tape the ends together and use them as napkin rings. You can get creative and use colored paper, stickers, or draw some decorations.

Make place cards! Take a piece of card stock and cut it in half. Fold each piece in half again. Write the name of each guest on one side and a joke or two on the other.

Give a performance! Ask your siblings or guests to join you to entertain the crowd. Take turns reading joke questions out loud and have the other answer the joke.

Team activity! Create two teams. Give each team a list of different jokes. Teams go back and forth telling jokes and get a point for every joke they're able to correctly answer. The team with the most points wins something.

Tips on How To Tell a Joke

- Practice reading the joke out loud a few times to help you remember it. You may want to practice reading in front of a mirror.

- Find a family member or friend and ask them if they want to hear a joke.

- As you tell the joke, remember to say it slowly and clearly so people understand every word.

- Adding a small pause helps to build up suspense and can make the joke even funnier.

- Deliver the final punch line. Remember to say it slowly, then wait for the laughs.

- If you mess up, that's OK. Move on and tell another joke. Remember, everyone loves jokes!

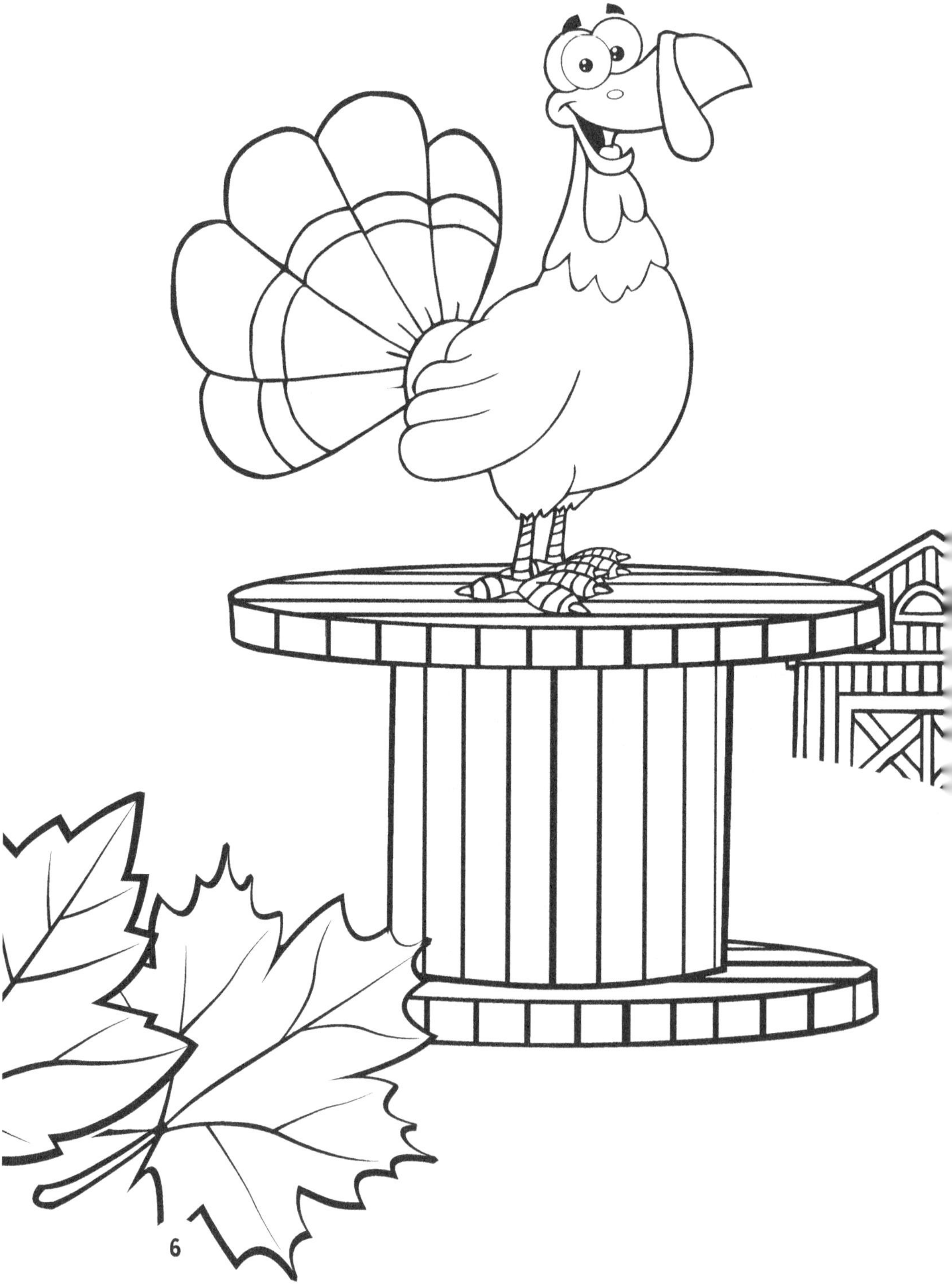

1

TURKEY JOKES

How do you tell the difference between turkeys and chickens?

Chickens celebrate Thanksgiving.

Why can't you take a turkey to Thanksgiving dinner?

They use fowl language.

Why didn't the turkey eat any pumpkin pie?

He was a little stuffed.

Why did the police take the turkey in for questioning on Thanksgiving?

They suspected fowl play.

What's the key ingredient at Thanksgiving?

The Tur-KEY!

Why do turkeys have terrible table manners?

Because they always go "gobble, gobble."

What do you call a running turkey on Thanksgiving?

Fast food.

What's a turkey's favorite website?

Google-google-google!

What are we most thankful for this Thanksgiving?

Not being a turkey.

Why did the turkey cross the road twice?

To prove he wasn't chicken.

What is a turkey's favorite dessert?

Peach gobbler.

If you call a large turkey a gobbler, what do you call a baby one?

A goblet.

How is a plushie
like a turkey?

They are both stuffed.

How does the turkey
drink its juice?

With a gobblet.

What do you call an odd
and unusual turkey?

A quir-key.

What do you call a
sarcastic turkey?

A smir-key.

What do you call an
over-caffeinated turey?

A per-key.

Why should you never set the turkey
next to the Thanksgiving pies?

Because he will gobble, gobble them up!

What happened to the turkey that got into a fight?

He got the stuffing knocked out of him.

What kind of weather does a turkey like?

Fowl weather.

What's the best dance to do on Thanksgiving?

The turkey-trot.

What's the best way to stuff a turkey?

Serve all his favorite food.

What is it called when a turkey fumbles in football?

A fowl play.

Why did the turkey sit on the tomahawk?

To try to hatchet.

What do turkeys like to do on sunny days?

Have peck-nics.

What do you call a turkey on the day after Thanksgiving?

Lucky.

What do you call it when a group of people takes turns making fun of the Thanksgiving turkey?

A roast.

TURKEY JOKES

What did the small turkeys tell the big turkey?

Peck on someone your own size.

What would you get if you crossed a turkey with an octopus?

Eight feather dusters.

What do you call a mean, dried-up turkey?

A jerky turkey.

What happened when the turkey met the axe?

He lost his head.

Where do you find a
turkey with no legs?

Exactly where you left it.

Why do turkeys make
bad baseball players?

They only hit fowl balls.

What is a turkey's
favorite tree?

The poul-tree.

What do you call it
when a family passes
down a turkey recipe?

Copy and basting.

What do you call a
turkey's twin?

A Gobblegänger.

How did they send the
turkey through the mail?

Bird Class.

TURKEY JOKES

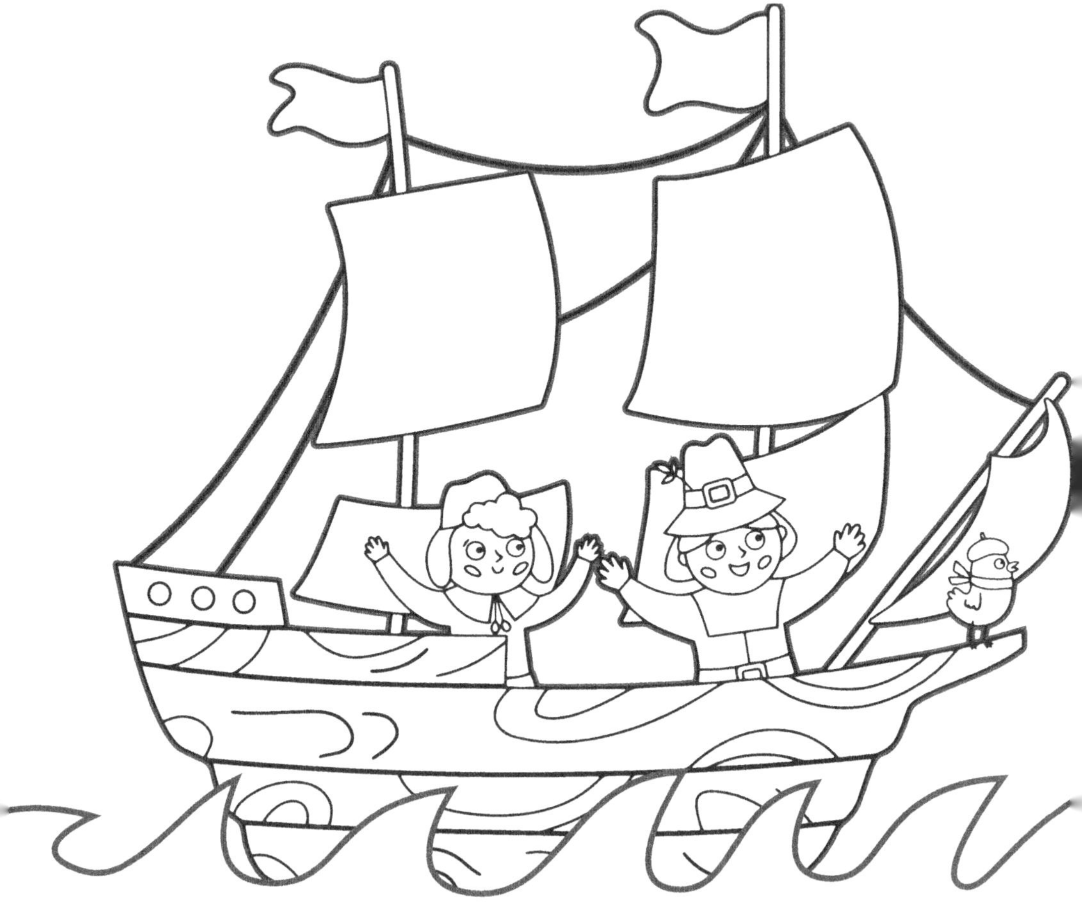

2

THANKSGIVING ORIGINS & TRADITIONS

During the first pilgrim landing, on what did they stand?

Their two feet.

Why did pilgrims smell good?

Because they were cologne-ists.

When did Americans start saying, "God bless America?"

When the first pilgrim sneezed.

How were pilgrims like ants?

They had a monarchy and lived in colonies.

Why did Columbus get lost?

Because the directions were not Pacific.

What type of transport brought the first pilgrims to America?

The Colum-BUS.

What came before the Mayflower?

The Aprilflower.

If April showers bring May flowers, what do May flowers bring?

Pilgrims.

THANKSGIVING ORIGINS & TRADITIONS

If pilgrims came on the Mayflower, on what did cows come?

The MOOOOO Flower.

During the journey across the Atlantic, what music did pilgrims play?

Plymouth rock.

Why did Columbus cross the ocean?

To get to the other tide.

What kind of tea did American colonists love?

Liber-tea.

What does the Statue of Liberty stand for?

Because she can't sit down.

At what time did pilgrim sailors eat dinner?

Mari-time.

What is a good pilgrim friend called?

A pal-grim.

Why didn't pilgrims tell secrets in their cornfields?

Because they knew corn had ears.

What did the pilgrim say when they landed on the beach?

"Shell, yeah!"

What do pilgrims say at Thanksgiving by the beach?

"This is the sea-son."

What did Columbus say at sea to inspire his men?

"Seas the day!"

How did pilgrim sailors greet each other?

"Seas and greetings!"

What did one flag say to another flag?

Nothing at all. It just waved.

What did the pilgrim wear to dinner?

A (har)vest.

Why do pilgrims' pants always fall down?

Because their buckles are on their hats.

Why didn't the pilgrim want to make the bread?

It's a crummy job.

THANKSGIVING ORIGINS & TRADITIONS

Why did the pilgrim cross the road?

Because he was chasing the turkey.

What's the smallest unit of measurement in the pilgrim cookbook?

Pil-gram.

What did pilgrims use to bake cookies?

May-flour.

3

THANKSGIVING FOOD & CELEBRATIONS

What veggie helps
tie your shoes?

String beans.

Why was the
Thanksgiving stew
so expensive?

It had 24 carrots.

What veggie is a sailor's
worst nightmare?

Leeks.

What did the guests say
after Thanksgiving?

*"Good pie, everyone
and good cluck."*

Why was the
herb surprised on
Thanksgiving?

He never saw it cumin.

What did the
puzzled corn say?

I am so corn-fused.

Why can't I tell you
about a rumor about
butter on toast?

You might spread it.

Why can't a farmer
trust her veggies
to keep secrets?

*Corn has ears, potatoes
have eyes, and beans
stalk around.*

Why was the
Thanksgiving band
unable to play their set?

*Because someone
ate the drumsticks.*

Which day of the week
do potatoes have
nightmares about?

Fry-day.

What does a mushroom
that needs help say?

"I'm in truffle!"

Why did the apple pie perform at the Thanksgiving dinner table?

It loved all the apple-ause.

What do you call beans that have been in the sun too long?

Baked beans.

What can you never eat for Thanksgiving dinner?

Breakfast or lunch.

What is a potato called when it wears glasses?

A spec-tater.

What do you get when you accidentally cross a pie with a snake?

A pie-thon.

Who makes the best banana splits?

Those who attend sundae school.

Why do potatoes make great detectives?

Because they always keep their eyes peeled.

What is a spud after a huge Thanksgiving dinner?

A couch potato.

Want me to make a veggie joke?

Oh, wait, no one would carrot all.

What's green, sings, and is perfect for a Thanksgiving party?

Elvis Parsley.

Did you hear about the man who tried to drink a load of gravy?

He was a laughing stock all night.

What herb never says yes?

Orega-NO!

What game do desserts play on Thanksgiving?

I s'pie with my little eye.

What side dish tells the worst jokes?

Corn(y) bread.

How do you like your apple pie?

Any way you spice it.

What's one good reason you should save Thanksgiving leftovers for tomorrow?

So it doesn't go to waist.

What is wise advice from rosemary?

That this sage pun was a long thyme cumin.

What always comes at the beginning of a parade?

The letter P.

THANKSGIVING FOOD & CELEBRATIONS

What do you call potato children?

Tater tots.

Why did the cranberries turn red?

Because they saw the turkey dressing.

What can you say to compliment a legume?

You are a great human bean.

Why didn't the chef add any herbs
to her Thanksgiving roast?

She didn't have the thyme.

Why are mushrooms the best veggies to hang out with?
They are the fungi-est guys.

Why should a casserole avoid sailing?
Because it can stew all over you.

What do butchers say at Thanksgiving?
"We supply the sausages to make ends meat."

What is the best sort of veggie pun?
Ones you can't beet.

What do you say to a student maize on his last day of school?

Corn-gratulations.

What did the baby corn say to the mom corn?

"Where's my pop corn?"

What did the pie crust say to the turkey?

I crusted you.

What did papa tomato say to baby tomato while they were out walking?

You should ketchup.

What rank would an ear of corn have in an army?

Kernel.

What do you call an important bean?

VI-Pea.

What do you say when
a pie is finished?

*"Another one bites
the crust!"*

What do mushrooms
say when a bus is full?

*"Please scoot over, as
there's not mush-room."*

What's a ghost's
favorite dessert?

I-scream.

Much like corn, why can't
you trust mushrooms?

They are stalk-ers.

THANKSGIVING FOOD & CELEBRATIONS

Why didn't the green bean answer the door?

It was in the can.

What's the best dance move to use
at a Thanksgiving party?

Twerkey-ing

Where does Christmas come before Thanksgiving?

In the dictionary.

4

THANKSGIVING KNOCK KNOCK JOKES

Knock, knock.
Who's there?
Arthur. Arthur who?
Arthur any leftovers?

Knock, knock.
Who's there?
Phillip.
Phillip who?
Phillip my plate.

Knock, knock.
Who's there?
Norma Lee.
Norma Lee who?
Norma Lee, I don't eat this much.

Knock, knock.
Who's there?
Watson.
Watson who?
Watson the program for Thanksgiving day?

Knock, knock.
Who's there?
Dewy.
Dewy who?
Dewy have to wait long to start Thanksgiving dinner?

Knock, knock.
Who's there?
Annie.
Annie who?
Annie body seen the pumpkin pie?

Knock, knock.
Who's there?
Tamara.
Tamara who?
Tamara we'll have Thanksgiving leftovers.

Knock, knock.
Who's there?
Gladys.
Gladys who?
Gladys Thanksgiving.

THANKSGIVING KNOCK KNOCK JOKES

Knock, knock.
Who's there?
Luke.
Luke who?
Luke at all this
Thanksgiving food!

Knock, knock.
Who's there?
Don.
Don who?
Don eat all the apple
pie. I want some more.

Knock, knock.
Who's there?
Emma.
Emma who?
Emma real pig when
it comes to eating pie
on Thanksgiving.

Knock, knock.
Who's there?
Esther.
Esther who?
Esther any more
cranberry sauce?

Knock, knock.
Who's there?
Harry.
Harry who?
Harry up, I'm hungry for Thanksgiving dinner.

Knock, knock.
Who's there?
Odette.
Odette who?
Odette's a big turkey.

THANKSGIVING KNOCK KNOCK JOKES

Knock, knock.
Who's there?
Sid.
Sid who?
Sid down. It's time to eat Thanksgiving dinner.

Knock, knock.
Who's there?
Diana.
Diana who?
Diana thirst over here. Please get me a drink.

Knock, knock.
Who's there?
Darryl.
Darryl who?
Darryl be enough pie for everyone on Thanksgiving.

Knock, knock.
Who's there?
Wilma.
Wilma who?
Wil Ma know to save the wishbone?

THANKSGIVING KNOCK KNOCK JOKES

Knock, knock.
Who's there?
Feather.
Feather who?
Feather last time,
please set the table for
Thanksgiving dinner.

Knock, knock.
Who's there?
Howie.
Howie who?
Howie going to spend
Thanksgiving?

Knock, knock.
Who's there?
Manny.
Manny who?
Manny guests are coming
for Thanksgiving dinner.

Knock, knock.
Who's there?
Nate.
Nate who?
Nate too much on
Thanksgiving last year...

Knock, knock.
Who's there?
Nadia.
Nadia who?
Nadia head if you want
more pumpkin pie.

Knock, knock.
Who's there?
Savvy.
Savvy who?
Savvy me the drumstick!

THANKSGIVING KNOCK KNOCK JOKES

Knock, knock.
Who's there?
Wanda.
Wanda who?
Wanda watch the
Thanksgiving parade?

Knock, knock.
Who's there?
Aida.
Aida who?
Aida lot more than
I should have for
Thanksgiving dinner.

Knock, knock.
Who's there?
Ben.
Ben who?
Ben nice spending
time with the family
at Thanksgiving.

Knock, knock.
Who's there?
Dez.
Dez who?
Dez-aster in the kitchen
when Dad tries to
make the gravy.

Knock, knock.
Who's there?
Franny.
Franny who?
Franny more gravy left?

Knock, knock.
Who's there?
Eddie.
Eddie who?
Eddie more pie and I'm going
to get a stomach ache.

THANKSGIVING JOKE BOOK FOR KIDS

5

THANKSGIVING PUNS & ONE-LINERS

My family told me to stop telling Thanksgiving jokes…but I told them I couldn't quit "cold turkey."

Orange you pumped for Thanksgiving?

Family, friends, food – it doesn't get any butter than this.

You think I'm done? Honey, you ain't seen stuffing yet.

I'm all about that baste.

Hey, I just met you, and this is gravy, but here's my stuffing, so carve me maybe.

You think you're crazy about Thanksgiving? Turkeys literally lose their heads at that time of year.

My mom was going to serve sweet potatoes with Thanksgiving dinner, but I sat on them. Now she's serving squash.

Did you hear about the conservative turkey? It has two right wings.

THANKSGIVING PUNS & ONE-LINERS

I've got my pie on you.

Go on, Pumpkin, bake my day.

Eat, drink, and be cranberry.

I yam what I yam.

Maize I have another, please?

You're the pumpkin pie of my eye.

Corn we all just get along and calm the corn-y jokes.

How can you dessert me when the evening has just started?

Thanks for pudding up with me.

Food puns pickle my fancy for loafing around.

The main dish for Thanksgiving this year is fowl.

THANKSGIVING JOKE BOOK FOR KIDS

6

FALL JOKES

What did the joking pumpkin say?

I'm a pun-king.

What did the tree say to autumn?

Please leaf me alone.

How do trees get onto the internet?

They just LOG on.

What did one autumn leaf say to another?

I'm falling for you.

Why do trees hate tests so much?

Because they get stumped on all the questions.

Why did the tree worry that he would never get his leaves back after fall?

He didn't be-leaf in himself.

What month does every tree dread?

Sep-timberrrrrrr!

Why do trees like to try new things each year?

Because every autumn they turn over a new leaf.

Why are trees so carefree and easy going?

Because every fall, they let loose.

What is the cutest season?

Awwtumn.

FALL JOKES

What is it called when a tree takes time off from work in autumn?

Paid leaf.

What happens when winter arrives?

Autumn leaves.

7

FALL KNOCK KNOCK JOKES

Knock, knock.
Who's there?
Theresa.
Theresa who?
Theresa green until fall.

Knock, knock.
Who's there?
Leaf.
Leaf who?
Leaf me alone!

Knock, knock.
Who's there?
Iva.
Iva who?
Iva bunch of leaves
that need raking!

Knock, knock.
Who's there?
Iowa.
Iowa who?
Iowa fire we could
all sit around!

Knock, knock.
Who's there?
Wool.
Wool who?
Wool you get me a
sweater? It's freezing.

FALL KNOCK KNOCK JOKES

Knock, knock.
Who's there?
Orange.
Orange who?
Orange you going to say hello?

Knock, knock.
Who's there?
Dawn.
Dawn who?
Dawn leave me out here in the cold.

Knock, knock.
Who's there?
Otto.
Otto who?
Otto listen to your parents and wear warm clothes.

Knock, knock.
Who's there?
Philippa.
Philippa who?
Philippa bathtub. I'm covered in mud.

Knock, knock.
Who's there?
Olive.
Olive who?
Olive looking at the different color autumn leaves.

FALL KNOCK KNOCK JOKES

THANKSGIVING JOKE BOOK FOR KIDS

8

FALL PUNS & ONE-LINERS

Let's just fall it a day.

Oh, my gourd. I love fall.

I slipped on a pumpkin today, and it caught me off gourd.

Wow, we've come fall circle this year.

It's fall coming back to me now.

Leaves during fall change their color autumn-matically.

Don't stop be-leafing in the magic of the season.

Are you oak-ay?
Yes, I'm pine.

Be-leaf in yourself.

I would never leaf you.

You really autumn know...

I would tell you
an autumn joke,
but you probably
wouldn't fall for it.

A tree had a fight
with autumn and said,
"That's it! I'm leafing!"

Orange you glad the
leaves are turning?

I'm so happy,
I could yellow
about it.

FALL PUNS & ONE-LINERS

Humpty Dumpty had
a great summer...
but a terrible fall.

Pumpkin spice and
everything nice.

Sorry I'm latte; I had to
get my pumpkin spice.

Fall leaves whenever
winter knocks
on the door.

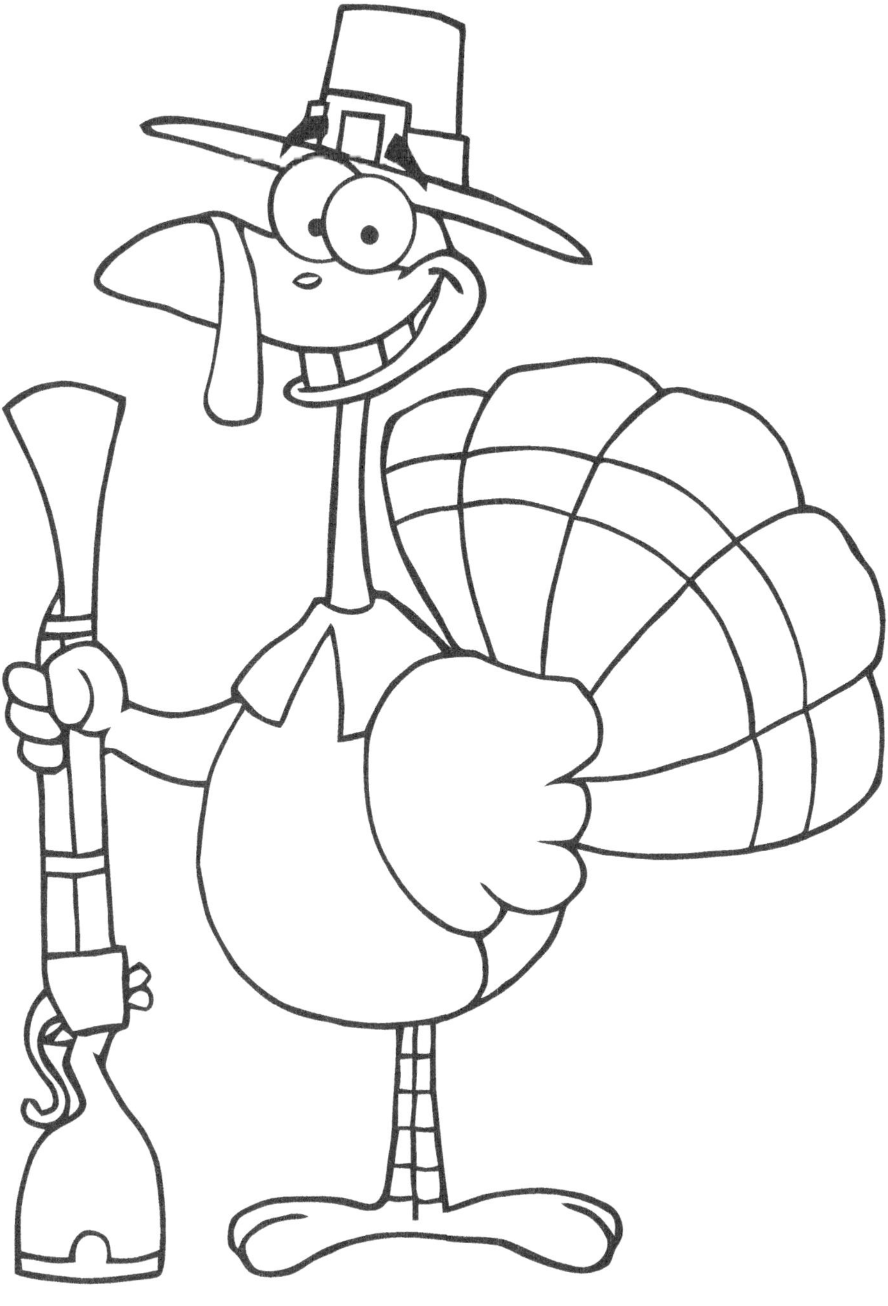

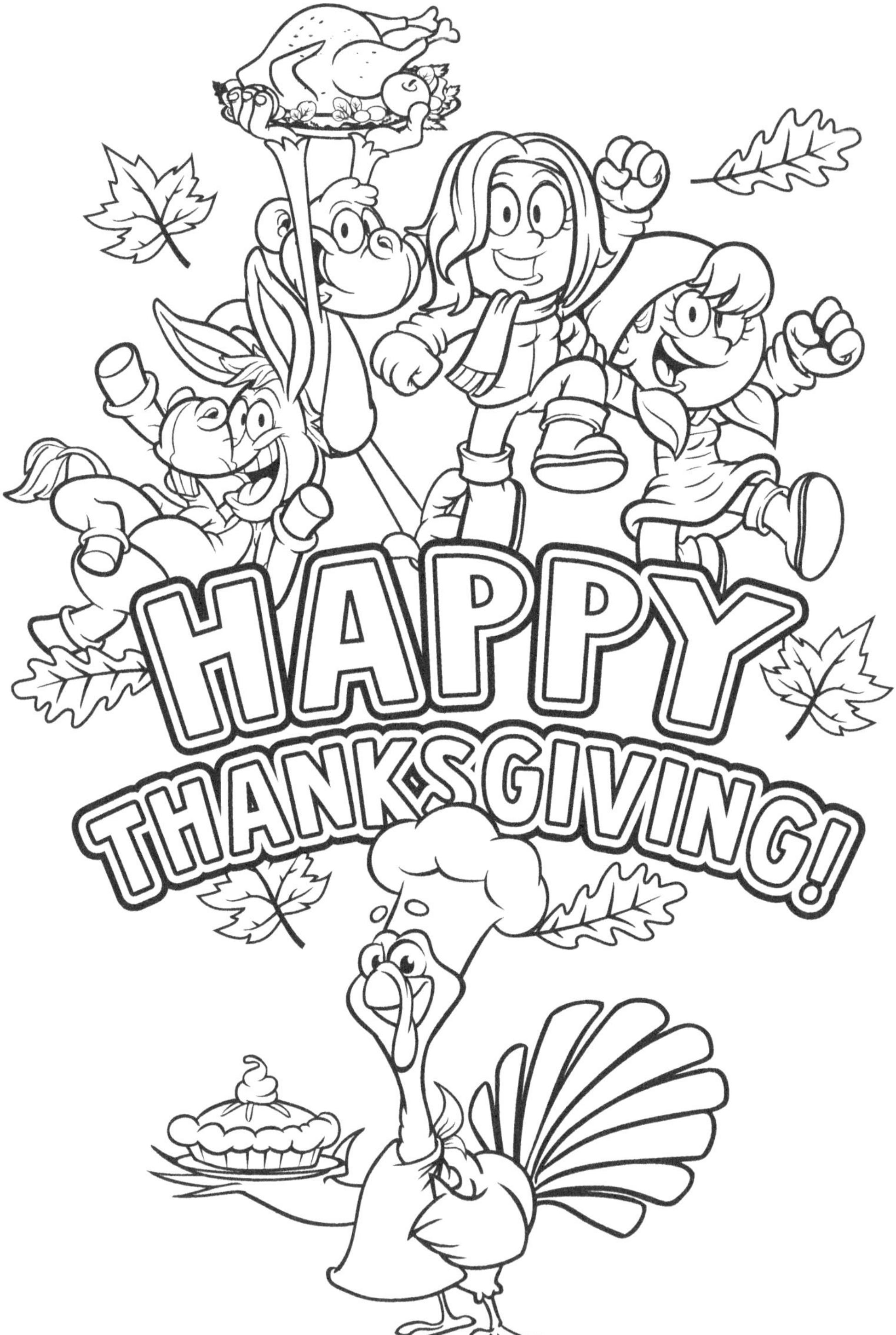
HAPPY
THANKSGIVING!

BEFORE YOU GO

Did you have fun with these sometimes corny Thanksgiving and fall jokes?

Now that you have gotten the hang of jokes, spend some time thinking up some of your own! Create your own jokes about fun things you like to do.

Once you think up your own jokes, you can play the game anywhere! It is a great game to play on long road trips, at school, or even when you are waiting in line at the grocery store.

Have fun coming up with your own jokes and endless giggles!

WRITE YOUR OWN JOKES!

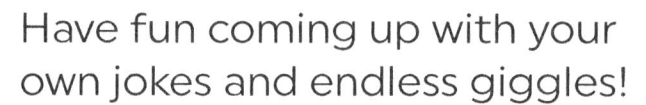

Have fun coming up with your own jokes and endless giggles!

WRITE YOUR OWN JOKES!

WRITE YOUR OWN JOKES!

WRITE YOUR OWN JOKES!

WRITE YOUR OWN JOKES!

WRITE YOUR OWN JOKES!

WRITE YOUR OWN JOKES!

WRITE YOUR OWN JOKES!

WRITE YOUR OWN JOKES!

WRITE YOUR OWN JOKES!

WRITE YOUR OWN JOKES!

WRITE YOUR OWN JOKES!

WRITE YOUR OWN JOKES!

WRITE YOUR OWN JOKES!

WRITE YOUR OWN JOKES!

COLLECT THEM ALL!

Thanksgiving Joke Book for Kids

Thanksgiving Would You Rather Book for Kids

www.riddlesandgiggles.com

REFERENCES

59 Top Hilarious History Jokes For Kids by Kidadl. (n.d.). Kidadl.com. https://kidadl.com/articles/top-hilarious-history-jokes-for-kids

75+ Best Autumn Puns To Fall In Love With by Kidadl. (n.d.). Kidadl.com. https://kidadl.com/articles/best-autumn-puns-to-fall-in-love-with

Duford, M. J. (n.d.). *Fall Puns: 101+ Autumn Wordplay Jokes That Will Leaf You Smiling*. Home for the Harvest. https://www.homefortheharvest.com/fall-puns/

Donovan, B. (2020, October 15). *These Funny Thanksgiving Jokes Will Be a Hit at the Kids' Table on Turkey Day*. Country Living. https://www.countryliving.com/life/a28522581/thanksgiving-jokes/

Green, A. (2020, August 1). *120 Colorful Fall Captions & Cute Fall Puns for Instagram*. Eternal Arrival. https://eternalarrival.com/quotes/fall-captions-puns-for-instagram/

Jester. (2017a, November 2). Corn Jokes | *Clean Corn Jokes*. Fun Kids Jokes. https://funkidsjokes.com/corn-jokes/

Jester. (2018c, November 18). *Thanksgiving Knock Knock Jokes | Clean Thanksgiving Knock Knock Jokes*. Fun Kids Jokes. https://funkidsjokes.com/thanksgiving-knock-knock-jokes/

O'Sullivan, K., & Donovan, B. (2021, July 30). *These Hilarious Fall Puns Are Almost Too Funny for Their Own Gourd*. Country Living. https://www.countryliving.com/life/a23326517/fall-puns-cute-funny/

Pun Generator | Random Name Puns Generator. (n.d.). www.pun-Generator.com. https://www.pun-generator.com/

Pilgrims Jokes. (n.d.). www.theholidayspot.com. https://www.theholidayspot.com/thanksgiving/jokes/pilgrims.htm

RhymeZone Rhyming Dictionary and Thesaurus. (2018). Rhymezone.com. https://www.rhymezone.com/

The 36+ Best Columbus Jokes - Upjoke. (n.d.). Upjoke.com. https://upjoke.com/columbus-jokes

Made in the USA
Monee, IL
05 November 2022